Jim Henson

Master Muppets Puppeteer & Filmmaker

by Grace Hansen

Abdo
HISTORY MAKER
BIOGRAPHIES
Kids

abdopublishing.com

Published by Abdo Kids, a division of ABDO, P.O. Box 398166, Minneapolis, Minnesota 55439.
Copyright © 2020 by Abdo Consulting Group, Inc. International copyrights reserved in all countries.
No part of this book may be reproduced in any form without written permission from the publisher.
Abdo Kids Jumbo™ is a trademark and logo of Abdo Kids.

Printed in the United States of America, North Mankato, Minnesota.

102019

012020

THIS BOOK CONTAINS
RECYCLED MATERIALS

Photo Credits: Alamy, AP Images, Everette Collection, Getty Images, iStock,
Seth Poppel/Yearbook Library, Shutterstock

Production Contributors: Teddy Borth, Jennie Forsberg, Grace Hansen
Design Contributors: Dorothy Toth, Pakou Moua

Library of Congress Control Number: 2019941230
Publisher's Cataloging-in-Publication Data

Names: Hansen, Grace, author.

Title: Jim Henson / by Grace Hansen

Other title: Master Muppets puppeteer & filmmaker

Description: Minneapolis, Minnesota : Abdo Kids, 2020 | Series: History maker biographies | Includes
    online resources and index.

Identifiers: ISBN 9781532188992 (lib. bdg.) | ISBN 9781532189487 (ebook) | ISBN 9781098200466
    (Read-to-Me ebook)

Subjects: LCSH: Henson, Jim--Juvenile literature. | Puppeteers--Biography--Juvenile literature. | Muppets
    (Fictitious characters)--Juvenile literature. | Fraggle Rock (Television program)--Juvenile literature. |
    Children's television programs--Juvenile literature. | Actors--Biography--Juvenile literature. | Puppet
    television programs--Juvenile literature.

Classification: DDC 791.53 [B]--dc23

Table of Contents

Early Years

James Maury Henson was born on September 24, 1936. He grew up in Leland, Mississippi.

Mississippi

The Rainbow Connection Bridge
In Honor Of Jim Henson

When Jim was around 10 years old, the family moved to Maryland. In high school, he joined a puppetry club. He was a fan of puppet TV shows, like *Kukla, Fran and Ollie*.

In 1954, Henson started college at the University of Maryland. That year he also created a puppet show. It was called *Sam and Friends*.

9

Sam and Friends starred a bald-headed puppet named Sam. Kermit was one of Sam's many friends. This character would one day become Kermit the Frog.

Muppets Take Form

In 1958, Henson **cofounded** Muppets, Inc. with his future wife, Jane. The company made its characters from **flexible** materials. This allowed the puppets to show many emotions.

Muppets, Inc. began creating characters for a new show set to air in 1969. The show was called *Sesame Street*. The lovable bunch included Big Bird, Cookie Monster, Bert, and Ernie.

Sesame Street was a giant success. It appeared on screens in more than 100 countries and in 14 languages!

17

In 1976, *The Muppet Show* aired for the first time. On the new show, Miss Piggy made her grand **debut**!

19

Death & Legacy

Henson helped create more children's shows until 1990. He died at the young age of 53. His children took over his work. His legacy and characters still bring joy to people today.

Timeline

Henson graduates from high school and enrolls at the University of Maryland. He makes his first television appearance.

The Muppets appear for the first time on the *Today Show*.

The Muppet Show begins its first season.

May 16
Jim Henson dies in New York City.

1954   **1960**   **1976**   **1990**

1936   **1955**   **1969**   **1979**   **1991**

September 24
James Maury Henson is born in Greenville, Mississippi.

Sam and Friends airs live for the first time in Washington, DC.

Sesame Street debuts with many lovable Muppets characters.

The Muppet Movie premieres.

Henson is honored with a star on the Hollywood Walk of Fame.

Glossary

cofounded – to have joined with one or more people to start something new.

debut – a first appearance.

flexible – easily bent without breaking.

legacy – one's work and efforts that live on and contribute to future generations.

Index

Abdo Kids
ONLINE
FREE! ONLINE MULTIMEDIA RESOURCES

Visit **abdokids.com** to access crafts, games, videos, and more!

Use Abdo Kids code

HJK8992

or scan this QR code!